Bigger and Smaller

Written by Larry Dane Brimner • Illustrated by Patrick Girouard

Published in the United States of America by The Child's World®
PO Box 326 • Chanhassen, MN 55317-0326
800-599-READ • www.childsworld.com

Reading Adviser

Cecilia Minden-Cupp, PhD, Director of Language and Literacy, Harvard University Graduate School
of Education, Cambridge, Massachusetts

Acknowledgments

The Child's World®: Mary Berendes, Publishing Director

Editorial Directions, Inc.: E. Russell Primm, Editorial Director and Project Manager; Katie Marsico,
Associate Editor; Judith Shiffer, Assistant Editor; Matt Messbarger, Editorial Assistant

The Design Lab: Kathleen Petelinsek, Design and Art Production

Library of Congress Cataloging-in-Publication Data

Brimner, Larry Dane.
 Bigger and smaller / written by Larry Dane Brimner ; illustrated by Patrick Girouard.
    p. cm. — (Magic door to learning)
 Summary: A girl and her younger brother learn the difference between big and small by comparing
themselves to various animals.
 ISBN 1-59296-532-6 (lib. bdg. : alk. paper) [1. Size—Fiction. 2. Animals—Fiction. 3. Brothers and
sisters—Fiction.] I. Girouard, Patrick, ill. II. Title.
 PZ7.B767Bkg 2005
 [E]—dc22   2005005367

A book is a door, a magic door.
It can take you places
you have never been before.
Ready? Set?
Turn the page.
Open the door.
Now it is time to explore.

A brother and sister
are at the zoo.
Hey, Big Sister, look
at me. I am bigger
than a hedgehog.

Don't you see?
I am bigger than a monkey.

I am bigger than a turtle.

A koala, a parrot,
or a pink flamingo?
Hah! None of *them*
is as big as me.

Hey, Little Brother,
look over there.
You are smaller than
that lion and
smaller than that bear.

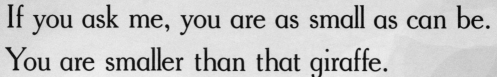

If you ask me, you are as small as can be.
You are smaller than that giraffe.

You would have to
stretch to reach its knee.
An ostrich, a bison, or
a two-humped camel?

19

Oh, Little Brother,
don't *you* see?
You are smaller
than them all.

And you are smaller than me!

Our story is over, but there is still much to explore beyond the magic door!

Who's bigger and smaller than you? Take a trip to the zoo and look at all the different animals. Which animals are larger than you? Which are smaller? Are any about your size?

These books will help you explore at the library and at home:

Gutman, Dan, and Jim Paillot (illustrator). *Miss Small Is Off the Wall!* New York: HarperCollins, 2004.

Silverman, Erica, and S. D. Schindler (illustrator). *Big Pumpkin.* New York: Maxwell Macmillan International, 1992.

About the Author

Larry Dane Brimner is an award-winning author of more than 120 books for children. When he isn't at his computer writing, he can be found biking in Colorado or hiking in Arizona. You can visit him online at *www.brimner.com.*

About the Illustrator

Little is known about illustrator Patrick Girouard, although rumors abound. It has been said that as a child he was struck by lightning and magnetized for a week. In addition to his artistic talents, he has the strength of ten men, can see around corners, and has the ability to talk to dogs. People have claimed that he lives in Missouri, Connecticut, Florida, New York, and Illinois, but he has been sighted most recently in Indiana. He is pen pals with Big Foot.